THE

The Poetry of Dorothy Bonarjee

THE HINDU BARD

The Poetry of Dorothy Bonarjee

EDITED BY
MOHINI GUPTA
and ANDREW WHITEHEAD

HONNO PRESS

First published by Honno in 2023
'Ailsa Craig', Heol y Cawl, Dinas Powys, Wales. CF64 4AH

© Estate of Dorothy Bonarjee, 2023
Introductions © Mohini Gupta and Andrew Whitehead, 2023

British Library Cataloguing in Publication Data

ISBN: 978-1-912905-78-2 print
ISBN: 978-1-912905-79-9 e-book

No part of this publication may be reproduced, stored in a retrieval system, or transmitted in any form or by any means, electronic, mechanical, photocopying, recording or otherwise, without clearance from the Publishers.

Printed with the financial support of the Books Council of Wales

Cover image: Dorothy Bonarjee, reproduced
by kind permission of Sheela Bonarjee
Cover design: Graham Preston
Printed by 4edge Limited

CONTENTS

INTRODUCTIONS	1
Love and Poetry in Aberystwyth *Mohini Gupta*	3
Dorothy Bonarjee, the 'Hindu Bard' *Andrew Whitehead*	13
A Note on the Texts	23
THE POEMS	35
Sense of Nature	37
Sense of the Past	61
Sense of Place	69
Sense of Love and Loss	83
Acknowledgements	97
A Note about the Editors	98

INTRODUCTIONS

LOVE AND POETRY IN ABERYSTWYTH

Mohini Gupta

Ri Khasi Ri Khasi, nga ieid ia pha,
Ka Ri ka ba ieid uba rim uba jah

I always begin my school workshops in Wales with a song. The song is 'Ri Khasi' – the Khasi anthem from the North East of India. 'Khasi' is a tribe of people from the state of Meghalaya in North-Eastern India, and the Khasi people are among the few Austro-Asiatic speakers in India. This song starts sounding familiar to every student in the classroom within a few seconds, and they realise it is set exactly to the tune of the Welsh national anthem 'Hen Wlad Fy Nhadau' (Old Land Of My Fathers), composed in 1856 by a father-son duo in Pontypridd.

India and Wales share a deep and complex history. This particular Indo-Welsh connection amongst the Khasi community can be traced back to the influence of Welsh missionaries in North Eastern India. The community is especially indebted to the Welsh since its spoken language, Khasi, was first written down as a script by the Welshman Thomas Jones. There are still parts of India that remain impacted by Welsh culture and tradition. The first time I learned of the National Eisteddfod – an 800-year old traditional festival in Wales celebrating poetry and music – and told my mother about it, she exclaimed, 'But our school used to run an Eisteddfod competition every year!' I was amazed that the Eisteddfod had made it to a girls' convent school in Pune (albeit with the English pronunciation of the letter 'f' as 'f', and not 'v' as in Welsh).

Comedians such as Eddie Izzard often mock the similarities between the Welsh and Indian accents, the sing-song tone of the two. What is less talked about in popular culture is the relationship between the Welsh and Indian languages – both belonging to the Indo-European family of languages. I found that it was easier to learn Welsh because of my knowledge of Sanskrit, Hindu and Urdu, rather than my knowledge of English (except, of course, for the inevitable loan words from English in the contemporary Welsh vocabulary). For instance, Welsh consonant mutations ('treiglad') were easier to understand through the Hindi consonant chart, which was arranged according to which part of the mouth was used while pronouncing them – a perfect phonetic explanation of the Welsh mutation system. I also identified deeply with Welsh language politics and in particular, its struggle to remain relevant against the coloniser's language, English. Practices like the 'Welsh Not' – where a small piece of wood was passed on in turn to students who were 'caught' speaking Welsh in order to punish the last student wearing it – had created generational trauma associated with speaking the Welsh language in school in favour of speaking English, and it was encouraging to see a renewed interest in the language amongst young people in some parts of the country, an attempt to move past the internalised shame attached to the mother tongue as a result of the fervent Welsh language movement since the 1960s.

As I continue to build on my deep love for and interest in Welsh culture and language, it turns out that I'm not the first Indian woman to have arrived in Aberystwyth and fallen in love with this coastal Welsh town. Exactly 105 years before I arrived in this town, there was another North Indian woman, also with a keen interest in poetry, who had immersed herself in the daily life of Aberystwyth. Dorothy Noel Bonarjee ('Dorf') belonged to an upper-caste, Bengali Brahmin, landed family in Uttar Pradesh, and was sent to England for her education at the age of 10. She preferred to attend university in Aberystwyth over London, and arrived there in 1912 with her brother (Whitehead, 2020). She continues to be the only woman of South Asian descent to have an entry in the Dictionary of Welsh Biography and to be celebrated as the University of Aberystwyth completes 150 years in 2022.

While she clearly possessed social and economic privilege in India, she struggled as a woman of Asian heritage at the Welsh university. She was rejected by her Welsh fiancé's family for being Indian. But this did not hold her back from becoming a prominent name on campus soon after she arrived. Not only was she involved in the debating and literary societies at the College, she also won the College Eisteddfod chair in 1914 with her lyrical ode to Owain Lawgoch, a Welsh soldier who served in the 14th century. Lawgoch was a descendant of Llywelyn the Great, a King of Gwynedd in North Wales known as the Prince of Wales in the 13th century. As a soldier he fought against England on behalf of the French. He had never lived in Wales but yet had a strong connection with the country and remained conscious of his hereditary claims as a successor of the two Llywelyns – Llywelyn the Great and Llywelyn the Last, one of the last native princes of Wales before the English conquest of Wales. The topic for that year's College Eisteddfod was Owain Lawgoch, so Dorf did not have a choice but to write on him, even though it is possible that she sympathised with his loyalty to the Welsh independence movement and also prophesied her own connection with France, where she was to spend the rest of her life. An excerpt from her chair-winning poem reads:

> He told him of the lonely rock-strewn shore,
> The dark, brown sea-weed lying on the sand.
> The wild black spirits of the storm, that tore
> The heart from out the water. And the land
> That lies in quivering, weary agony
> Beneath the lashes of the thundering waves.
> But sometimes when the nights are still and fair
> The water ripples softly round the caves.
> And peace falls from the stars on land and sea,
> Sweet peace down-falling through the dew-filled air.
> (Published in *The Dragon*, March 1914)

The fact that an English-language poem won the College Eisteddfod was in itself an exceptional achievement by Dorf, along with being the first woman of colour to win it. Unfortunately, the rest of this 200-line poem appears no longer to exist in the archives of the university or the National Library of Wales – also an indication of her lack of attachment to the poem as it is not found in any of her archived documents. Dorf continued to publish a series of scattered poems in Welsh journals like *The Dragon* and *Welsh Outlook* over the next few years, but an entire collection of her poems has never been published before. Some of the poems in this collection are unpublished verses jotted down by her in a little black book, which has been preserved by her dear niece and closest surviving descendant, Sheela Bonarjee, who has been kind enough to share her work with us. Sheela currently lives in Leicester and remains enthusiastic about sharing Dorf's love for poetry and Wales with the world. She speaks fondly of their relationship and of a special trip that they took to Aberystwyth together in the 1970s, many years after Dorf had moved to France with her then-husband. She visited her friends on this trip and spoke to Sheela about her love for the town at length.

Bonarjee's poetry can be described as vivid and rich, full of pathos and evocative imagery. She employs rhyme in some poems, while some have been written in blank verse. Her poems are mostly concerned with nature, nostalgia, childhood, love and loss, making them reminiscent of Romantic poets like Wordsworth, Shelley, or Yeats. Consider the following definition of the Romantics (Forward, 2014):

> The Romantics renounced the rationalism and order associated with the preceding Enlightenment era, stressing the importance of expressing authentic personal feelings. They had a real sense of responsibility to their fellow men: they felt it was their duty to use their poetry to inform and inspire others, and to change society.

Bonarjee's work was in keeping with this definition of Romantic poetry; she excelled at expressing 'authentic personal emotions' in her poetry. Based on the themes in her poems, this collection has been divided into four sections: Sense of Nature; Sense of the Past; Sense of Place; and Sense of Love and Loss. Dorf has a gift for drawing you into her world and making you perceive the intimidating beauty of Nature through her eyes. She has the ability to create elaborate, moving pictures of nature and then sometimes end the poem with a surprising twist that grounds the poetry in her own life. Read, for instance, her poem titled 'The Grave in the Woodland' which describes nature for two stanzas and then ends with:

> Where the Dawn is cold and white
> With the sorrow it has known;
> In the haunted gloom-filled woodland
> Lies a small grave all alone, –
> In the shadowy, dim woodland
> Lies my Childhood – all alone.

She creates a sense of gloom associated with nature in the poem and ends it on a note of grief, as she mourns a childhood forlorn and lost. Her honesty and rawness in the poems are what make them so poignant. She has also used rhyme and repetition to drive home the feeling of being 'all alone'. Dorf creates powerful visual-scapes in most of her poems. Consider the vibrant imagery in the lines 'A loveliness supremely wrought / The incalculable sky / And to its wondering heart it caught / And held the burning stars' from the poem 'The Pool'. It is also reminiscent of the imagery in Yeats' 'The Song of Wandering Aengus' (1899).

Much like early Romantic poet William Blake's collection *Songs of Innocence and Experience* (1789 and 1794), some of Bonarjee's poems are also rooted in the locations she has experienced and bring out her knack of painting a picture of the urban scenes around her.

Her 'London' poem from 1916 describes 'rows of dazzling windows, and vague flight of carriages, and rapid, furtive cars'. Compare Blake's poem with the same title from 1794 which reads 'I wander thro' each charter'd street, / Near where the charter'd Thames does flow / And mark in every face I meet / Marks of weakness, marks of woe'. Dorf's poem on 'Solleis Ville, Provence', where she lived the later part of her life after marrying French artist Paul Surtel, vividly refers to 'The brown-roofed houses' which 'seem / A flock of huddled sheep, seen in a dream.'

Not only do the themes in her poems echo voices of canonical Romantic poets, her language at times takes on a Pre-Raphaelite turn in its language and themes. There are multiple references to Greek and Roman goddesses as in 'Epstein's Venus'. In the poem 'Summer 1914', she addresses a fictional Glycera ('the laughter-loving one') saying, 'Dost thou remember Glycera, the light?'. Who is Glycera and why is an Indian poet in Wales writing about her? At the same time, this is also not surprising for someone who had been educated in England since the age of 10, and probably was also trying to fit in culturally.

Given our shared connection with India, I was on the constant look-out for influences from India or Indian languages in her poetry. According to Sheela, Dorf must have spoken a bit of Hindustani – an amalgamation of Hindi and Urdu before their linguistic boundaries were so distinctly drawn, and the lingua franca of Northern India and Pakistan before the partition of the two nations at Independence. It was a struggle to find traces of her Indian roots in her poems, except for a fleeting reference to 'the little Indian shawl lying on the chair' in her poem 'Afterwards' from 1915. I noticed a repetition in the lines, 'Was that a singing bird? Or just my heart that *listening listening* hears the call?' (italics mine) in the poem 'Enchanted Garden'. While this could be a mistranscription by the author, to me this sounds like a direct translation of the Hindi phrase *'sunte sunte'* or 'listening listening' (meaning 'while listening'). This would be a very commonly spoken phrase in colloquial Hindi. In fact, this shows up in another poem, 'L'éternité, C'est Le Temps De L'extase', in the line '*All all* that glory' (italics mine) to emphasise the 'all' of the glory – once again, a very characteristic form of repetition for emphasis prevalent in Indian languages. There is also a cryptic reference to 'the land of the Jonokies' in the poem 'The Gods', which could possibly refer to Janaki, the other name for the Hindu goddess Sita, one of the central figures from the Sanskrit epic 'The Ramayana'. This is followed by a reference to 'the land of the Mergriffvins', which is possibly a Welsh neologism, and this may be true of 'Jonokies' as well, but it is difficult to believe that the character of Janaki did not inspire this line.

I believe that her poetic voice is at its most commanding in her poems on love and loss. Consider the painful tone in her poem 'You said once I was lucky', which could be about a lover but could also be addressed to her brother:

> You said once I was lucky, but you wouldn't say it now;
> You swore that fortune never came your way;
> You used to say I always scored – well, now your turn is here
> You must confess that you have won today.

The theme of loss comes up again in her brilliant poem 'Renunciation': 'So I must give thee up – not with the glow / Of those who losing much yet rather gain. / But losing all'. She also compares her feelings of loss to a feeling of having descended to hell in 'Arrogance':

> But when your little frightened soul had fled
> And all your glorious radiant lies were dead
> I laughed again because you knew I fell
> Where God had never passed – in hell.

There seem to be multiple references to a broken heart in her poems and this has been portrayed extremely powerfully in her verse. They are not always romantic – her poem about her son who passed away as an infant is brief, candid and moving. She is a master of being vulnerable in her verse and laying out all her emotions beautifully and honestly through her words. The sections in this collection enable us to understand how she came to terms with her questions of her own identity and social position and continued to grapple with the answers as she grew older. We follow a young, passionate Dorothy until she becomes the wise and mature woman who has experienced loss and pain intimately.

This collection seeks to bring forward Dorothy's poetry to the public for the first time ever. In a world where women continue to struggle to make their voices heard, Dorothy's is unique. She occupied a complex social position which provided her with caste and class privileges in India, but also disenfranchised her as a gender and ethnic minority in England. She was the first woman to get a law degree from University College London; she participated passionately in the suffrage movement of the time, and befriended anti-war figures in Aberystwyth in the early 20th century. Her involvement in the British suffrage movement puts her in the same league as Indian women in Britain such as Princess Sophia Duleep Singh, Bhikaji Cama, and Cornelia Sorabji, and it has been recorded that their participation in this movement was also linked with demands of independence from the Empire (Mukherjee, 2018). In this sense, this collection could be seen as a slice of history – of India, of England and of Wales during the time of the First World War – in which a woman on the one hand was granted the independence to study (a luxury not many women of her time could boast of, whether in India or in England), and on the other hand struggled to claim her independence in personal, professional and political spaces. But intriguingly, her poetry does not betray her politics – it seems to be reflective mostly of her deeper emotions and a contemplation on her surroundings, whether natural or urban, making it seem almost like a deliberate choice. This brings her even closer to the Romantics than she may have intended, and makes her a compelling literary and political figure to be studied further.

I owe my gratitude to Andrew Whitehead, who discovered this story through Sheela Bonarjee, wrote about it after extensive research, and invited me to collaborate on this collection as someone who might understand Dorf's unconventional love for Aberystwyth and poetry as we share a similar Indo-Welsh journey. In all these years, I have never believed in the theory of reincarnations, but this serendipitous story has made me reconsider.

I imagine Dorf would have become an adept Welsh speaker too, if she had stayed on in Aberystwyth longer instead of moving permanently to France. I'll end with the last three lines of Dorf's Bardic chair-winning verse, with my translation of them into Welsh:

Gorffwys yw Marwolaeth. Mae Mawredd yn cysgu am ysbaid –
A dyma'r nos – ond wedi hynny daw'r Wawr
I oleuo pob lle gyda'i phelydrau euraid.

Death is a rest. So Greatness sleeps a space –
And this is night – but after comes the Dawn
With golden rays to lighten every place.

References:

- Blake, William. 1926. *Songs of Innocence and Experience*. London: Ernest Benn.
- Forward, Stephanie. 2014. "The Romantics", The British Library. https://www.bl.uk/romantics-and-victorians/articles/the-romantics. Accessed October 11, 2022.
- Joshi, Sopan. 2017. "The Wonderful Izzard." *India Today*, April 1, 2017. https://www.indiatoday.in/magazine/leisure/story/20170306-eddie-izzard-stand-up-comedian-cross-dressing-985878-2017-04-01. Accessed July 1, 2022.

- Mukherjee, Sumita. 2018. *Indian Suffragettes: Female Identities and Transnational Networks*. New Delhi: Oxford University Press.
- Price, Watkin William. n.d. "James, Evan." In *Dictionary of Welsh Biography*. Accessed August 28, 2022.
- "St. Xavier's Hr. Sec. School Umoid, Meghalaya – Student Handbook." n.d. Accessed July 2, 2022. https://stxaviersumoid.com/wp-content/uploads/2020/08/2020-SXHSS-Handbook-web.pdf.
- "The Welsh Not." n.d. A History of the World. BBC and the British Museum. Accessed July 1, 2022. https://www.bbc.co.uk/ahistoryoftheworld/objects/j35VCjYcS0CC3RGzvkLb-Q.
- Whitehead, Andrew. 2020. "'She Is Beautiful but She Is Indian': The Student Who Became a Welsh Bard at 19." *BBC News*, December 28, 2020. https://www.bbc.co.uk/news/stories-55430717. Accessed July 1, 2022.
- Yeats, W. B. 1899. *The Wind among the Reeds*. London: Elkin Mathews.

DOROTHY BONARJEE, THE 'HINDU BARD'

Andrew Whitehead

Dorothy Noel Bonarjee was born in India, brought up in England and married in France – but it was in Wales in the years just before and during the First World War that she developed as a poet. Her most celebrated achievement – being chaired at a prestigious Eisteddfod while still a teenager – is notable above all because she was so obviously not Welsh. She became known, not entirely accurately, as the Hindu Bard. That was both her claim to fame and a burden too, as it carried the implication that her verse was remarkable not so much for its own merit as for the acculturation of its composer. This volume, the first collection of Dorothy Bonarjee's poetry, demonstrates the scale of her accomplishment, and suggests that her success at an Eisteddfod gave her the confidence which allowed her to develop as a poet. Over the course of seven years, nineteen of her poems were published either in the college journal, *The Dragon*, or in *The Welsh Outlook*. When her association with Wales ceased, so did her poetry. She wrote a little in later years but not with the same verve and none of her later work seems to have been published. She clearly took pride in her poetry and kept a collation of her verse, published and unpublished, in a battered black notebook that was bequeathed to her niece, Sheela Bonarjee. Without that black book, this book could not have been assembled.

Throughout her life, Dorothy Bonarjee was an outsider. She seems to have sought out that sense of being different, or perhaps she didn't know where she could fit in. In India, her family stood apart by class, culture and religion. They were upper-caste Bengali brahmins but Dorothy spent her early childhood on an estate inherited by her mother hundreds of miles away from Bengal in Rampur, then a princely state, to the east of Delhi in North India. She was born in the nearby town of Bareilly in April 1894.

Dorothy was related to one of the commanding figures in the early endeavours to give political expression to Indian nationalism. Womesh Chunder Bonnarjee (the spellings are inconsistent and are a deviation from the more standard anglicisation of this common Bengali surname as Banerjee) was a barrister who qualified at the Middle Temple in London and who in 1885 presided over the first session of the Indian National Congress. Congress developed from an elite group advocating a greater role for Indians in their own governance to become, in the following century, the broad-based nationalist movement which led India to independence.

Dorothy's own branch of the family headed off in its own idiosyncratic direction. Her grandfather, Shib Chunder Bonarjee, was converted to Christianity as a young man by a celebrated Scottish missionary, Alexander Duff. He entered the ministry and became pastor of the Scottish Church in Calcutta (now Kolkata). Both Dorothy's parents were among the small number of upper class Indian Christians. But in Rampur they led a fairly simple life. One of Dorothy's brothers remembered the family home as desperately remote: 'in the wild, with no amenities and little companionship'.

Dorothy's life changed utterly in 1904 when – along with her brothers, Bertie and Neil – she was sent to London for her education. She was just ten years old. She seems never to have seen India again. A photograph published in Neil's memoirs depicts the three young Bonarjees at about the time they arrived in London. Dorothy looks demure in a white dress with a black ribbon in her hair (Bonarjee, opposite p. 48). Bertie, her older brother, is in a suit and tie. It's a statement of how English they had become even though the world around would always see them as Indian. Dorothy's parents – both of whom had spent time in Britain – wanted their children to be part of India's England educated elite who were carving out a greater role in running the country. Neil Bonarjee later remarked that in India, "England-returned" gained 'something of the snob value of a peerage in Great Britain' (Bonarjee, 21).

Dorothy's father, Debendra Nath Bonarjee, was a barrister as well as a landowner who prided himself in his interest in his tenants' welfare. She was probably closer to her mother, Janet Anna Bonarjee (née Sirkar), who was a strong advocate of girls' education and while in London was the honorary secretary of the Indian Women's Education Association. The family set up home at Dulwich. The boys attended the renowned Dulwich College; Dorothy went to Dulwich High School for Girls. The parents eventually returned to India leaving their children in London, and in the 1911 census the three young Bonarjees were listed as living in the Dulwich home of a Calcutta-born and Cambridge-educated barrister, Joseph Boyle, who had become a private tutor. The household was strikingly global: Boyle's wife was from Mauritius; his sister-in-law, step-son and step-daughter were all born in India; one of the two other student boarders was from the Canaries; and the servants were two young women from Bombay.

The pioneering Congressman W.C. Bonnarjee had similarly divided his time between London and India, establishing a household in Croydon and educating his children there. Two of Bonnarjee's daughters, Susila and Janaki, studied at Newnham College, Cambridge. The example of another wing of the family, and perhaps the insistence of her mother, allowed Dorothy a privilege rare for a woman in either Britain or India at the time: the opportunity to go to university. The family had expected Dorothy to take a place at the University of London. But according to family folklore, she found London too 'snobbish' and so opted instead for the University College of Wales in the largely Welsh-speaking seaside town of Aberystwyth. 'Where the hell is that?!' her father is said to have exclaimed. But Dorothy got her way and was admitted to Aberystwyth to study French in 1912. Her brother

Bertie, perhaps not quite as scholastic as his sister, also enrolled there in part to serve as chaperone.

Dorothy's decision may well have been shaped by the progressive reputation of the college. The University College of Wales at Aberystwyth – the oldest of three colleges then forming the University of Wales – would then have had about 400 students. Students from outside Wales made up at most one-in-five of the student community. From its foundation in 1872, the college was open to students of all religious persuasions and cultural backgrounds. It also had an impressive record on gender equality, as it accepted women for the same courses as men from 1884. By the time Dorothy arrived there, nearly half the students were women, a much higher proportion than at most British universities at this time. At her graduation ceremony in 1916 – when many of the men were fighting in Flanders and France – women were in a clear majority.

The number of overseas students at Aberystwyth was modest. Across Britain at the time of the First World War, there were about a thousand Indian students at British universities, though only perhaps fifty or so would have been women. Dorothy Bonarjee and her brother must have been conspicuous at the college, but they were not unique in having Asian heritage. One of the marshalls at their degree ceremony was a student from Java.

Dorothy was clearly a popular student, taking a prominent role in the literary and debating society and helping to edit the college journal. She stayed in Alexandra Hall on the promenade, which opened in 1896 and was Britain's first purpose-built women's hall of residence. Two group photographs depict her as at the centre of activity rather than on the margins. Her big moment came in February 1914 at the college's annual Eisteddfod. All poems were submitted under pseudonyms and could at that time be in Welsh or English. The *Cambria Daily Leader* reported on its front page under the headline 'Hindu Lady Chaired' the 'remarkable' scenes when the winner was announced:

> The highest place was awarded to 'Shita', for an ode written in English, and described as an excellent and highly dramatic treatment of the subject ... Miss Bonarjee received a deafening ovation when she stood up and revealed herself as 'Shita'. She was led up to the throne ... The 'chairing' ceremony then proceeded amidst great enthusiasm. (*Cambria Daily Leader*, March 2, 1914)

Dorothy's parents, making their first visit to Britain in four years, were present to see their nineteen-year-old daughter's success. Her father was prevailed upon to address the crowd, thanking them for the way they had 'received a successful competitor of a different race and country'. If India had given birth to a poet, he declared, Wales had educated her and given her an opportunity to develop her poetic instincts (*Times of India*, March 21, 1914).

Dorothy Bonarjee was the first foreign student and the first woman to triumph at the college Eisteddfod. To add to the prestige of her success, the adjudicator was T. Gwynn Jones, a towering figure in Welsh literature. Another eminent Welsh writer and academic, T. H. Parry Williams – who in 1912 had been the first person to be both crowned and chaired at the National Eisteddfod – conducted her to the stage for the chairing ceremony. She was in exalted company.

Her triumph was widely celebrated, including in *Y Wawr* [The Dawn], a new Welsh-language magazine at Aberystwyth which sought to challenge the cautious conventionality of *The Dragon*. It offered congratulations to 'Miss Dorothy Bonarjee – Rhiain India', which can be translated as 'a maiden of India' (*Y Wawr*, March 1914). The ripples reached as far as India's national newspapers with reports in both the *Times of India* and the *Statesman*. India's increasing cultural influence had been reflected the previous year when another Bengali, Rabindranath Tagore, became the first Indian to win the Nobel Prize for Literature. By coincidence, the bardic chair at the college Eisteddfod at Bangor was also won that year by a woman, but it was not until 2001 that a woman was chaired at the National Eisteddfod.

Entries for the bardic chair had to follow a specified metre and style and to address a given topic, in this case the fourteenth-century Welsh warrior Owain Lawgoch. Perhaps because of these prescriptions, Bonarjee doesn't seem to have regarded the winning verse as one of her best. It's not included in the notebook in which she assembled much of her poetry. While brief extracts were published in *The Dragon* which lauded 'a poem full of imaginative fire and relieved by passages of wonderful descriptive power', the full text of the Eisteddfod-winning ode appears not to have survived (*Dragon*, March 1914). The whereabouts of the hand-carved oak chair she would have received is also not known. But her success was not out of the blue. She was reported to have come close to winning the chair the previous year as well.

Emboldened by her achievement, Bonarjee began to contribute poems to a newly established monthly journal, *The Welsh Outlook*, an expression of increasing national self-confidence which both reflected and encouraged incipient Welsh cultural nationalism. But her student years were overshadowed by war. Bertie, her brother, enlisted and, after the completion of his degree, served in France where he helped to liaise with Punjabi troops fighting on the Western Front. The war years were turbulent in Aberystwyth. A number of longstanding German residents of the town were hounded out. Among them was Carl Hermann Ethé, the college's longstanding Professor of German and Oriental Languages who would have been known to the Bonarjees. In October 1914, he was confronted by an angry mob. He left Aberystwyth and never returned. Alongside the jingoism there was also a strong anti-war movement, partly linked to the strong Christian religious background in Wales at that time, and both T. Gwynn Jones and T. H. Parry Williams were openly critical of the war.

To judge from her verse, Dorothy steered a middle course, reflecting the pain of war but not repudiating the war effort of which her brother was part. In November 1914, Dorothy Bonarjee and a colleague led a 'sing-song in the Gymnasium' at Aberystwyth, the proceeds from which were 'for the benefit of our Indian troops' (*Dragon*, December 1914). When in July 1916 Dorothy and her brother were awarded their degrees at the annual congregation at the Coliseum Theatre in Aberystwyth, the impact of war was evident. 'Several of the degree men appeared in khaki and were cheered and a large number of degrees were conferred in absentia because the men were away serving their King and country in the war', according to a local paper.

Dorothy Bonarjee also endured a very personal wartime anguish. Alongside the poems she collated is a note, jotted down probably many years later but in her hand: 'Written at the age of 22 when a Welsh student after 3 years of secret engagement dropped me because his parents said "She is very beautiful and intelligent but she is Indian."' Dorothy's niece, Sheela Bonarjee, recalls her Auntie Dorf confiding about that failed romance: 'It destroyed her; she was distraught.' The poem which reflects that wound is 'Renunciation':

> So I must give thee up – not with the glow
>   Of those who losing much yet rather gain.
> But losing all. Did never martyr go
>   Along the bleeding road of useless pain?

While Dorothy may have relished being an outsider, there could be a painful price to pay for being different. Her younger brother, Neil, later studied at Oxford and came across a wall of prejudice there. 'Indians in general, it must be said, along with other coloured races were not popular in the University,' he wrote. His English fellow students 'had something which I had not, namely an Empire. They possessed, while I only belonged.' (Bonarjee, 41)

From Aberystwyth, Dorothy and Bertie returned to London where both took another degree course. Once more, she was a trailblazer. In 1918, she became the first internal woman student at

University College, London, to be awarded a law degree. Women were only allowed to practise law in the United Kingdom the following year, though Dorothy never sought to take advantage of this victory for women's rights. During the war years, her mother once again lived in London. In 1919, both women were signatories of the Indian's Women's Franchise Address which demanded that women in India be given the vote alongside British women who had been awarded a restricted franchise the previous year. Neil Bonarjee chronicled somewhat disapprovingly that his sister 'eagerly' observed the activities of suffragettes and imbibed 'other mildly radical influences' and mixed 'in minor artistic and literary circles considered "advanced" for the period.' (Bonarjee, 59)

The family expected that their offspring, once qualified, would return to make their lives and careers in India. Dorothy's brothers dutifully got on the boat; Dorothy herself rebelled. She was caught between different cultures and social values. She was free-spirited and committed to women's equality and not someone who would easily consent to a marriage arranged by her family in India, which would have been the expectation on her return. So she eloped with a French artist, Paul Surtel. Her father was furious; her mother seems to have been more understanding. The couple married in France in March 1921 by which time both parents were sufficiently reconciled to indicate to the British consul that they consented to the marriage. Dorothy and Paul settled in Provence. Surtel gained distinction as a painter; his wife largely retreated from public view. Even the accolade of a short article devoted to her poetry and complimentary of it, and encouragement from the poet Laurence Binyon and the literary scholar A.C. Bradley, failed to rekindle her writing (Das, 50-53).

Bonarjee's early years in France were marred by tragedy. She and Surtel had two children, a son, Denis, and a daughter, Claire Aruna. Denis died in infancy. By the mid-1930s the marriage was over. 'Nothing is more wearing morally than a weak husband', Dorothy commented many years later. Her family pleaded with her to return to India. Once again she refused. It was a decision she may later have regretted. Her father eventually bought her a small vineyard, Jaubergue, near Gonfaron in Provence, to serve as both home and livelihood. Her mother came out and lived with her in France for several years. During the Second World War, according to the family's account, Bonarjee took considerable risks in shielding Jewish children, on one occasion using her dead son's papers to provide a convincing back story. Both her parents died in India in the early 1940s and the war frustrated any wish Dorothy might have had to say farewell.

After the war, money was tight. Dorothy remained in France, lived a rather spartan life and never remarried. Sheela Bonarjee followed in her aunt's footsteps from Rampur in India to London in the 1950s. They were kindred spirits and Sheela made several visits to the south of France. She remembers her Auntie Dorf as elegant, confident and unconventional. In some ways she was very French, Sheela recalls: 'She had wine with every meal, which for me as an Indian was very strange and at times I wondered why I was so sleepy all day.' Dorothy spoke French with a pronounced accent but managed to cross cultural boundaries with ease. On occasions she would delight her French neighbours by dressing up in a sari. But she was in many ways more French, more English, perhaps even more Welsh, than she was Indian.

Dorothy Bonarjee kept in touch with some of her Welsh friends all her life. In old age, she made a final pilgrimage to her old university accompanied by her niece. She lived to within a few months of her ninetieth birthday. She has had the posthumous distinction of becoming the first person of Indian origin to be included among the thousands of entries in the *Dictionary of Welsh Biography*. Dorothy's daughter, Aruna, died in 2009. She has no direct descendants, and it's particularly fitting that her black notebook and other papers are to be deposited by her family at the Llyfrgell Genedlaethol Cymru / National Library of Wales at Aberystwyth.

References, bibliography and links (all sites accessed on August 30, 2022)

- Auchmuty, Rosemary. 2008. 'Early women law students at Cambridge and Oxford', *Journal of Legal History*, 29/1, pp. 63-97
- Bonarjee, N.B. 1970. *Under Two Masters*, Calcutta: Oxford University Press.
- Chapman, T. Robin. n.d. 'The breaking of *The Dawn*: the rise and decline of Aberystwyth students' first Welsh language magazine, *Y Wawr*'
  https://www.aber.ac.uk/en/media/departmental/informationservices/pdf/specialcollections/Y-Wawr-by-Robin-Chapman.pdf .
- Das, Harihar. 1922. 'The Poetry of Dorothy Noel Bonarjee', *Indus*, November, pp. 50-53
- Husbands, Christopher T. n.d. 'Professor Carl Hermann Ethé (1844-1917): also a victim of the First World War',
  https://www.aber.ac.uk/en/media/departmental/informationservices/pdf/Professor-Carl-Hermann-Eth%C3%A9.pdf
- Jenkins, Beth R. 2020. 'Bonarjee, Dorothy Noel', *Dictionary of Welsh Biography*, https://biography.wales/article/s12-BONA-NOE-1894
- Mukherjee, Sumita. 2009. *Nationalism, Education and Migrant Identities: the England-Returned*, Routledge.
- Norbury, Katharine (editor). 2021. *Women on Nature: an anthology of women's writing about the natural world in the east Atlantic archipelago*, London: Unbound.
- von Rothkirch, Alyce. 2009. 'Visions of Wales: *The Welsh Outlook*, 1914-1933', *Almanac*, 2009 visions-of-wales-almanac-june-2009.pdf.pdf
- Whitehead, Andrew. 2020. 'Dorothy Bonarjee: Bard of Aberystwyth', *Planet: the Welsh Internationalist*, 238, pp. 70-76
- Whitehead, Andrew. 2020. '"She is beautiful but she is Indian": the student who became a Welsh bard at 19', BBC News, 2020 https://www.bbc.co.uk/news/stories-55430717
- 'The Hindu Bard' a radio documentary on the BBC World Service, December 2020 https://www.bbc.co.uk/programmes/w3ct1d0z

A NOTE ON THE TEXTS

The poems that follow constitute the greater part of the published work of Dorothy Bonarjee and some of her unpublished verse. They have been chosen by the editors because of their merit or, in a few cases, because of the light they shed on the author's life. The selection is based substantially on the black notebook in which Bonarjee collated much of her poetry. This notebook contains more than forty of Bonarjee's sixty-five or so extant poems. Many are hand-written on slips of paper and pasted in. There's frustratingly little in this black book that offers any context for Bonarjee's writing. Indeed, it's not clear when in her life she assembled this selection, though a few jottings in French suggest that it was after she moved to France.

Published poems have been included as printed, even if Dorothy later made revisions by hand. Poems hitherto unpublished are given in what the editors understand to be the final version and the plus sign and ampersand have been rendered as 'and'. All ellipses are as in the original; in a few cases, the punctuation of hand-written poems has been standardised. In the case of untitled poems, the first line of the poem has been used in square brackets to stand for its title.

Dorothy's parents, father standing behind mother, Cambridge, about 1906

Dorothy and her older brother, Bertie, probably taken in India

Dorothy in London with her younger brother, Neil

Dorothy Bonarjee, in the striped blouse, while at Aberystwyth

Dorothy, front row, second from right, while at Aberystwyth
(Aberystwyth University Archives)

Bertie Bonarjee, front left, at Aberystwyth

Dorothy Bonarjee with her son Denis, 1922

Dorothy Bonarjee with her daughter, Claire Aruna

Dorothy Bonarjee, undated

Sheela Bonarjee as a young woman

THE POEMS

SENSE OF NATURE

NOON[1]

Noon! deep, languid light, that quivers in the sky
And fires the gorse-clad hills to throbbing gold.
One pale distant spire. A seagull's cry
That wakes dim echoes – but to sleep once more.
A valley steals down to the rock-strewn shore
And dreams in cool content of things long told;
This is a place of dreams, of drowsy fields
Of moon-filled haunts, and level yellow sands
Of little worn, grey houses by the road
Where dwell those who with strong, enduring hands
Untied the knot of life; whose patience yields
To death alone; who walking 'neath a load
Of sacrifice and silent thought for years
Have found sweet peace for all their bitter tears
By shadowy waysides and bowed, aged hills
Who know the secret, tender night fulfills
The promise of the glowing, fragrant noon.

---

[1] *Welsh Outlook*, July 1914. Later published retitled as 'Clarach' in *The Dragon*, March 1915. The Clarach is a small river which flows into the sea at Clarach Bay, north of Aberystwyth.

THE GRAVE IN THE WOODLAND[2]

In the silent woodland
Where the snow leaves fall and the light
Is grey and weary with the shadow of the night:
In the sleeping woodland
Where vague dreams moan
In a hopeless undertone,

Where the Dawn is cold and white
With the sorrow it has known;
In the haunted gloomfilled woodland
Lies a small grave all alone, –
In the shadowy, dim woodland
Lies my Childhood – all alone.

---

[2] *Welsh Outlook*, December 1914. Dorothy later renamed this poem 'Vale' and in a handwritten note wrote of it: 'To Rampore in memory of my childhood'.

A NIGHTMARE[3]

A dream not wholly seen; half vague, half clear;
Of straight dark corridors, not evil yet,
But strange, alluring in a hostile way,
You creep among them, wondering if you fear
The black, close hangings into which are set
Pale unresponsive mirrors, where you seem
A thing of smoke, a shadow thinly grey
That wavers past. You almost feel you dream
But are afraid to wake. A sudden turn
And then, a staircase, subtle like a snake;
The slow stairs crawling upward have no end
But wander on till you can scarce discern
Their steadfast ranks. ... You know you are awake
You whisper dully that no dream could send
This rushing, strangling horror. Then you see
A figure by the stairs. You dare not flee
But dragging hopeless feet, know all the while
That he is watching with cold, murderous eyes,
And craving with red lips, and satyr's smile,
And clenching fleshy hands. Your spirit dies
For you can feel his calculating eyes.
You cannot look behind and break the strain
For he is watching, watching from below
And smiling. And the terror in your brain
Becomes a madness, suffocating, dense.
You feel a wild, unreasoning panic grow
You cannot run or scream or look behind,
But shuddering climb, in wordless grim response ...
A little flickering breath of midnight wind

---

[3] *The Dragon*, December 1915

Falls on your face. And with a grasping cry
You run, and run – and wake.

                                       And over there
Are windows darkly blue, and in the sky
One low-poised star, aloof, remotely fair.

TO DIANA[4]

Oh! I will build a little world, of grass and wind and daisies,
A little laughing world for you where I can sometimes creep;
Of thistledown (just like your hair) and laughter and clear dewdrops,
With sunlight for your daytime eyes, and twilight for your sleep.

And you shall dance upon the hills with hurrying shadow cloudlets,
And run with lovely butterflies and play with baby things,
With lambs and bright-eyed furry mice and kittens and grass-hoppers,
And understand in your wise mind the song the blackbird sings.

And when you're tired of playing alone I know just where we'll wander,
We'll find out where the sun runs off and where the white stars go,
And where the dog's bark hides itself, and where the fairies gather.
Oh! I will build a world for you that only we two know!

---

[4] *Welsh Outlook*, July 1919

IMMENSITY[5]

Today a little wind is in the grass
So dim you hardly see it pass
　Or feel its faint soft lips.
　Yet, if you part the slender bright grass-tips
And stopping look quite silently awhile,
　You see small insects swiftly file
Along mysterious twisting ways,
　Like men in some great thick-meshed forest's maze,
Where closely woven branches hide the sky
　And giant trees toss terribly.
So do the grasses toss and sway
　And giant blades shut out the day.

---

[5] *Welsh Outlook*, July 1919. This poem is also included in an anthology *Women on Nature*, edited by Katharine Norbury and published in 2021.

SOLITUDE[6]

Solitude; two fallen glasses lying
The red wine trickling slowly on the floor
A few pale roses dying
She once wore.

Solitude; too hopeless for vain weeping
A candle's shuddering flame, no other light.
Another's lips are keeping
Pierrette tonight.

---

[6] Also entitled 'Solitude (To a Picture)'

FEAR

A shadow on a cloudless day;
No shape – but just a little nameless thing
That follows, follows at my play,
And looks at me with dreadful eyes.
No shape – but just a little silent thing,
Whose formless horror chokes my cries,
And slowly drugs my hopeless heart.
No shape – but just a little hellish thing,
That creeps behind and never will depart,
That looks at me quite silently,
All night and day it looks at me.

[DEATH HOLDS THAT HOUSE I KNOW]

Death holds that house I know.
Poor little house, so still,
With one light burning low
And blinds drawn to the sill
So decently, as though
No sad task they fulfil
Why do you stare?
I know that death is there
For in that room
Half-hidden in the gloom
The dead quiet body lies,
With weighted eyes
And folded hands and hair.

THE POOL

I passed a pool all willow hung
Where silence brooded with deep eyes
So still it was it almost seemed
It never could have sung.
Deep in its heart the white stars gleamed
Like trembling fireflies.

Yet through the calm triumphant day
It watched the lustrous woods rejoice
While Nature lived her perfect hour
Of beauty ere decay
And joined her flaming song of power
With sweet untroubled voice.

But now it lay in ecstasy
And saw between the leafy bars
A loveliness supremely wrought
The incalculable sky
And to its wondering heart it caught
And held the burning stars.

THE DAY

Dost thou remember Day O Day of light
The indecisive pallid hours ere night
Had fled? and dawn was but an old desire
A tired longing ghost with eyes of fire.
The discontent of birth that gives not life
And life's fierce joys, nor yet the quietness
Of death. The hopes that mocking truths betray
The irony of purposeless blind strife
The pain of watching dreams die effortless –
Dost thou remember these O steadfast Day?

So proud thou art and solemn in thy power
Thy destiny complete. Thy smallest flower
Its frail perfection gives to perfect thee
The humblest bird song swells thy harmony
How changed thy fear and troubled unbelief!
What vast divine content unfolds thee now!
The peace of longings solved and understood.
I cannot look unmoved on this small leaf
That light-filled sways above for it is thou
A flawless feast of some eternal mood.

The light ensnares my eyes yet in my brain
There old uncertain hours stir in pain;
And I am but a thought blown on the breath
Of some great spirit's laughter, seeing death
As storm crushed seaman knowing all is lost
Yet draws some comfort from a star's white beams
Being something fixed in that disordered scene.
Could I twixt light and darkness vainly tread
But find the wakening of those sightless dreams
As thou has found thyself, complete serene.

How gladly would I lose myself in thee
No discord but a throbbing ecstasy
Of song or fragrance or a wave of light
Small in myself great in thy ardent might.
Here where still trees a green gold whisper are
And quietness broods as a dove content.
And time lies sleeping 'neath the austere wings
Of stern Eternity. To see afar,
Faced from self's fearful lying irritant
Truth's changeless flame deep in the heart of things.

SONG

    O delicate pale may tree
Shake down your frail snow-petals upon her tenderly
White are your shimmering flowers, but whiter far is she
        O little laughing may tree

    Like soft-winged butterflies
Fall petals, through the blue air upon her where she lies
And stare the vivid green grass, and kiss her dreaming eyes
        Like faery butterflies

FANTASY

Now floating down the high walls of the sky
The ardent veils of noon the earth enfold.
A bright clear patterned image is the world
In a lake's deep watery mystery
And time and self in shoreless space are hurled,
In whose unfathomable dust-starred gold
My thoughts like birds in eager happiness
Cleanse their dimmed wings in purifying light.
And like an empty husk my body lies
Quiet in this elemental quietness.
In tremulous swift flight my thoughts arise
Blue throbbing purple, gold and radiant white
Save one who by my body sits apart
With folded scarlet wings, and tears my heart;
It never stirs, nor ever faintly sings,
Nor looks aloft where all the rest have flown,
But secretly with folded haunting wings,
By my deserted body, sits alone.

[TODAY A LAUGHING WIND IS IN THE TREE]

Today a laughing wind is in the tree
Where swings my blackbird merrily
And arrogantly sings
With sunlight on his wings
And from his swaying height looks down on me.

THE FOG

A fog wrapt all the town today
In fold on yellow loathsome fold
I crept along the perilous way
My eyes quite blind with smoke and cold.
While all around a company
Of phantom sounds marched up the streets.
I felt them passing close to me
And keeping time to my heart-beats;
Now loud, now dim, now rumbling bass –
And suddenly a thin young cry,
Then sound on sound in tumbling chase,
Then silence – then a falling sigh.
The fecund blankness thickly stirred
And sounds were frantic everywhere.
I could not see – I only heard
Tumultuous movement in the air.

And all the day it was the same ...
But when I left the town behind
A secret tide of silence came
Across the worn strand of my mind.
The quiet mist swayed on the breeze
And like a shadowed moon-stone seemed.
I saw elusive slender trees
Wave where its blue heart subtly gleamed.
And from the shrouded shifting deep
My cottage loomed in friendly sight.
Like some primeval beast asleep
In the grave watches of the night.

DEBUSSY'S LITTLE SHEPHERD[7]

Little laughing shepherd
Piping to the golden day,
Far across the scented fields
Piping clear and sweet.
Can you hear the faery bells
Calling, calling, you away
Calling "follow, follow, follow"
To your dancey feet

Little sleepy shepherd
Sitting on your grassy mound
Piping to your curly lambs
And dreamy mother sheep.
Can you hear the heather bells
Ringing gently all around
Ringing softly, gaily, dimly
Calling you to sleep

---

[7] Debussy's 'Little Shepherd' was part of a suite first performed in 1911.

THE HUNTRESS

The leopards hunt tonight,
The terrible, swift leopards of the moon.
Soon
Upon the mountain height
You'll hear their cries,
And see
Between the trees' black bases
Red stealthy stars,
Their burning eyes.
Through desolate ways
In tireless maze
The subtle leopards creep.
Before them flee
The ghosts of her dead lovers endlessly
Like dead, blown leaves
Her dead, pale lovers are.
And from afar
Her spells she weaves
While her fierce leopards leap
And track with cunning tread
The loveless dead.
Like wind-swift flame
The leopards hunt their game
And they are out tonight
Upon the mountain height.

[DEEP AND STILL ARE THE WOODS IN THE AUTUMN]

Deep and still are the woods in the autumn:
Enchanted like old forests in a tale;
Or wrapped round in a dream;
And full of silent water –
Lying motionless –
That holds the twisted branches sometimes
  On a fragment of pale sky
  Or even a bright star.
Deep and still are the woods in the autumn.
Tired a little of all their knowledge;
Weary of spring's young beauty and summer's fulfilling,
Proud and secret they stand.
And I who love them and know their familiar ways
Am afraid and dare not enter.
For they are still and profound as unheard music.
And I am afraid my heart will be caught like a star
In the captive water,
And see no more the happy happy spring,
And sing no more.
But lie quietly for ever in the brooding woods
  Lie for ever in the silent water
  A dream of the coming night
  And forget the coming dawn.

THE NIGHTINGALE[8]

   The sleeping fountains are stilled,
   So white in their ravished serenity
   That they are made of moonlight spilled
   On the soft dark night of the lawns.
And the pale translucent obscurity
Is aglow with remembered dawns.
   Each tree drips light from off its leaves;
And every shadow weaves
A magic net about the enchanted earth
And space is an ardent moon-lit scheme,
   Where God's immortal dream
Flowers from birth to death, from death to birth.

   O voice from out of the stillness!
   Dark lover of silence and the dewy night;
   Your ageless song partakes
   Of man's bright vision of loveliness.
   Behind the heavy veil of mortal sight,
Trembling with doom and beauty, Psyche wakes
Poised lovingly for dangerous Godward flight.

---

[8] Inscribed: 'To my mother'.

DAWN

When silence lies on the world,
Like the warm consolation of a bird's wing
On the pale mysterious world;
Then leave your *unquiet* desire and come with me
On the high roads, mute with dawn's prophetic beauty.
To shrouded vineyards adream of their awakening
Where clustered purple sweetness,
Downy swollen sweetness
Hides its glory trembling with foreknowledge
Or ruthless hands and press
(How sparkling flows the wine blood!)
O scattered loveliness!
Walk softly dear dreamer of my dreams, and speak not lest a word
Should bruise our hearts trembling with foreknowledge
Of slow destructive years
(How darkly flows the heart's blood!)
O unappeasing tears!
O brooding vines was that the wind that stirred?

CHRISTMAS SONG FOR JAUBERGUE[9]

Last night I heard the hills commune
  With white ecstatic stars and tune
Their million voices to the Voice
  That is the source of song.
And all the happy hills that rise
Ungathered to the beaming skies
Their fervid longing to rejoice
Appeased in joyous throng.

And all the laughing valleys too
About their mother mountains drew.
And sang ahead so high, so low
All through that wondrous night
And all because a Babe once lay
In Bethlehem so far away;
In Bethlehem so long ago
A Babe lay crowned with light.

The air was full of whisperings,
And sudden flash of radiant wings.
And God in all his glory shone
So none was unaware.
And gentle angels stooped to bless
The earth in blissful tenderness.
And every heart and tree and stone
Knew God is everywhere.

---

[9] Jaubergue was the name of Dorothy Bonarjee's vineyard and home in southern France.

SENSE OF THE PAST

THE GODS[10]

Should you ask me whence these stories,
Whence these legends and descriptions,
Telling of the Lit. and Deb. nights,
Telling of attempted speeches,
Drowned by yells and witty comments,
By fireworks and aimless laughter,
Loud as thunder in the mountains; –
I should answer, I should tell you
From the Coll. that stands in Aber,
From the land of the Jonokies,
From the land of the Mergriffvins,
Where that spirit – gentle Rumzee
Plays amongst the boots and benches.
I repeat them as I heard them
When I saw in Aber. College
All the Gods let loose together.
If still further you should ask me
Saying – "Come, my son, and tell me
Who are they these Gods of Aber?
Come they from the starry regions,
From the islands of the Blessed?"
I should answer your inquiries
Straightway in such words as follow:-
"Go on Friday to th' Exam Hall,
Where the orators are gathered.
Entering softly, go in silence
To the farthest, darkest corner.
Soon you'll hear sweet strains of music.
Howls and laughter rise together,

---

[10] *The Dragon*, December 1913

Quite regardless of the speaker,
And you'll see your next-door neighbour
Shut his ears and murmur sadly
"Ah! the Gods have come!"

                    My father,
Ask me not to tell you of them;
Rather go yourself and hear them;
Then returning homewards, ponder
On these strange Gods thus encountered,
And remembering their politeness,
Their excessive, great, politeness,
Thank your stars you are a *mortal*.

SUMMER 1914[11]

Dost thou remember Glycera, the light?
The pale clear morning light across the sky;
The fresh caress of early dawn; the flight
Of tangled waters flashing swiftly by;
The shimmering radiance of white mists that break
The ecstasy of flowers half awake
That open dew sprayed petals to the sun.
Dost thou remember Glycera, the light
  Dear laughter-loving one?

Dost thou remember Glycera, the light?
The fragrant murmurous light of afternoon;
Red poppies heavy-eyed, the vague delight
Of languid half-traced dreams that die so soon
As they are caught; swift shadow clouds that pass
In merriment across the cool-cheeked grass
The laughing grace of shepherd boys who run
Dost thou remember Glycera, the light
  Dear laughter-loving one?

Dost thou remember Glycera, the light?
Wherein the haggard world that holds thee now
Thy sad feet stumble and the weary night
Blinds thy happy eyes, and thou
Alone, in frightened anguish with bowed head,
Dost weep among the stern uncaring dead.
Still dance the shepherd boys beneath the sun ...
Dost thou remember Glycera, the light?
  Dear laughter-loving one?

---

[11] Dorothy noted that this poem was 'written in 1916'. Glycera or 'the sweet one' was a common name among women entertainers in ancient Greece.

EPSTEIN'S VENUS[12]

White Venus looked with anger in her eyes
And on her red bewildering lips the scorn
Burned to a flame; and in the vivid morn
Her laugh revealed a thousand mysteries.
Before her stood the pale appalling thing
Of lively curves; a crude essential shape
From whose blind nakedness was no escape
So elemental, terribly unseeing.
She smiled and saw the sunlight on his breast
And smiled again and saw her gleaming side
And in her strange deep eyes, the colour leapt.
She raised her arms in splendid swift unrest –
But ere the proud divine desire had died –
She looked – and shuddered suddenly –
                                      and wept.

---

[12] Jacob Epstein's marble sculpture of Venus was shown in 1917.

L'ÉTERNITÉ, C'EST LE TEMPS DE L'EXTASE [13]

Eternity! right at the journey's end you say?
A hard gained rest, a quiet unstirred ease?
The ship that all the winds of time have tired
Sleeping at last, in that unruffled sea
Where God's breath dies to silence.

And all those old heroic dreams? are they all dust?
Those green seas running past enchanted shores?
Those mortal lovely cities built by men
Who brood on steadfast things
All all that glory, all that proud endeavour
Where is the living thought that gave them form?
Those fire swept dreams, those lonely calvaries
Heart aching skies, unutterable dawns
Are they all thwarted by this deathly calm?

Eternity? ah no! it's this
A life; a day, a moment's ecstasy,
Immortal joy behind all mortal acts.

Eternity? I knew it all that day
Through all those sunlit hours shared with you
My dear, my heart's own friend.
Those laughing hours of mutual happiness
And blithe companionship.

"Fade slowly wistful light upon the hills
Our joy has made you brighter
Come quickly twilight shadows in the valley

---

[13] The title translates as 'eternity is the time of ecstasy'.

That I may lead my dear one to his house
And wrap him with my love's protecting wings
And care for him and serve him
And crown myself with his contentment".

Eternity, it's this: those gracious hours watching over you
And feeling your mute joy.

"Shine splendidly white stars and fill the valley
With austere loveliness, and let night's silence still
All earthly murmurs now
That I may seek my lover and my king.
Now all my dreams and dreaming
Now all my flights and wandering
Now all my love and longing
Find rest within his arms".

Eternity! it's this: this timeless bliss
This long-desired death, this radiant birth.
The dreamer and the dream are now consumed
And only Joy is left – divinely pure
And God has buried his lover's mortal heart
In his own ecstasy.

SENSE OF PLACE

PEASANTS[14]

Here once our houses stood, beside the fields
Some see drear ghastly relics, standing bare,
And weep for lofty homes; and sorrow yields
To vain regrets for treasures once so dear;
Wise ancient books, and pictures famed and rare
Yet there is hope for them in this despair
For they may see new treasures, and the fear
Of utter loneliness is never theirs.
What have we left? Our houses were our friends;
They smiled with us, and understood our cares.
Our fathers made them, and their memory lends
A passion to our lives. We have their dreams,
We labour as they did; and all our days
Are but the shadows of their far-off ones
That fall on us; and everywhere it seems
Their silent spirits wander. So life plays
With death. What now remains? We are alone.
This loss is greater far than life, it stuns
Our minds; we cannot think, nor feel, nor speak.
Those little careworn houses were our own;
We loved each step of them. They were so meek
In their simplicity; they held the tale
Of our unvarying lives within their walls.
O distant happy days, through which we strayed
With steady, slow-paced feet. Can we prevail
Against this deeper loss? What spell recalls
Past hopes? Can we take up the broken thread
Of our poor lives? For this great price we paid
Shall we have peace, or envy for the dead?

---

[14] *The Dragon*, November 1914. Also entitled 'France 1914'.

AFTERWARDS[15]

At last I am alone. I hear their feet
Drag slowly down the gloomy, silent street,
Until the fitful echoes die away.
The house is very still. All through the day
Sad figures stole along the stairs and wept,
And whispered lying useless words to me
Of Dawn and Resurrection; then they crept
Across the grey stone path, and through the gate.
It is so still – and I am all alone.
I dare not close my eyes for then I see
Your gravely smiling face; you seem to wait
As you have always done, to welcome me.
This fragrant room that once you called your own
Speaks but of you. The pictures on the wall,
The flowers, and books, the little Indian shawl
Lying on the chair. Now I am here alone,
And in my brain there is no thought nor fire,
Only a vague monotonous desire
To sleep. You were the sum of all the things
That made my life. They wept vain foolish tears
And told each other wisely that Time brings
Some healing with the thoughtless patient years.
I laughed at them. Oh God! it is so still –
I think some cord has broken in my brain.
I hear the clock's dull sinister refrain,
And wonder if this loneliness can kill.

---

[15] *Welsh Outlook*, January 1915

AT THE PLAY[16]

Look deeply where the gloom less darkly lies
Their fascinated, staring, eager eyes;
Their tense thrilled faces. You can see
Their absolute surrender. Motionless.
You can feel their strained intensity.
They look in breathless, deep, unconsciousness.
They have forgotten. See how they smile.
Outside the grey rain waits them; the dull street;
The slow procession of poor joyless days.
But here life enters not. For this short while
They laugh at truth, denying their defeat,
As through the darkness, silently they gaze.
Ah! The curtain falls, and swift lights burn
The veils from dreaming brains ... And far below
A murmur stirs, and languid women turn
To criticise each other, and to show
Their graceful charms. And here they lightly say
They want to *live*. And there – they want to play.

---

[16] *The Dragon*, March 1915

LONDON[17]

Light! deep orange, yellow, staring white,
And sudden banks of gloom – the lights again,
And rows of dazzling windows, and vague flight
Of carriages, and rapid, furtive cars,
And lamps that flicker past like falling stars,
And people everywhere. A deep refrain –
A solemn, never-ending undertone.
And mingled with its roar, in lighter vein,
The echo of incalculable feet.
To one who wanders midst the lights alone
There is a power in the throbbing street,
A beauty in the City's painted face,
And healing in the wisdom of her eyes.
And dear to him in that great heedless race,
In shame, and sorrow so forlornly wise
Whose secret good no sin can e'er efface.

---

[17] *Welsh Outlook*, January 1916

SUBURBAN HOUSES[18]

The houses in the towns are very wise;
Not with the kindly wisdom old-age brings –
Cottages have this, that stand alone
And look upon the road with peaceful eyes;
But with a silent wisdom of their own,
A dull acceptance of all men and things.
They learn it from each other. Through long days
They stand in two straight weary rows and stare
Across at one another, with a gaze
Of sombre dead indifference. If they speak
It is at night when all the blinds are drawn,
And street lamps only glimmer everywhere;
And then their voices are so tired and weak
That they soon die in silence. They are born
With this half-haunted, half-complacent air,
They never are alone, but always so
They gaze across, each in a thoughtful row.

---

[18] *The Dragon*, March 1916. Also published in *Welsh Outlook*, October 1917.

THE RETURN [19]

Now down my street slow footsteps come.
On either side the sleepless houses are
Who listen, dumb.
While from afar
Come sad remembering feet
Down my pale street.

O little sober houses, near your dead,
Who, from their graves on distant battle grounds
Forlorn, have fled.
Now dimly sounds
A murmur past each gate,
So desolate.

---

[19] *The Dragon*, June 1917

DANCER

A vast deserted stage
All black behind the footlight's glow
And now a little dancer, whom I know
In that great sombre cage.

On exquisite curved feet poised motionless
Now drifting on the violin's distress
In slow dreaming motion, now afire
With all their wailing passionate desire
Elusive gleaming arms, white subtle form
A snowflake whirling in a mid-night storm,
A moon-lit quivering leaf and now a star
Serene behind the footlight's yellow bar.

And eager eyes that gaze,
A hundred eyes all looking where
Behind the lights, so delicately fair
A little dancer sways.

LIGHTS

In Baker Street the lights hang in the air
Like gathered moons that politely stare
In wise remoteness from their clouded height.
In Westminster a mellow fancy broods
Amid fantastic fawny woods
Where yellow oranges gleam every night.
And often in the Strand there are I know
Alluring Christmas trees aglow
Each little tree decked with a ruby light.

I sometimes think the unforgetting dead
    From their reflective mansions fled
Like sad moths drifting beat their tragic wings
    Around the lights in mournful ecstasy.
Through wistful hours of evening
They haunt the town's familiar glimmerings
And till the morning passionately stray
About each well remembered way
And greatly long for kindly human things.

NON OMNIA MORIAR[20]

When I am dead I wish my soul could be
A little light on some swift London car
A little yellow light forever free
In ways familiar.

These old unwearied streets with me would share
Their solemn secret loveliness and I
Would see beneath the city's piteous glare
Her unstained majesty

I think I still shall dream, when I am dead
Of brooding houses and dim London skies
And my dead ears will hear far overhead
The newsboys' shrill young cries.

---

[20] The title translates as 'Not Everything Dies'.

THE CAFE

Inside the Café there was noise and glare
Cheap gilt and mirrors flashing everywhere
And crowded tables marble-topped. Grey smoke
Hung densely in a swaying dusky veil.
Swift looks and laughs and lips to passion spoke
And it was hot and tired and very stale.
But oh! outside the autumn night was sweet
And Piccadilly wistfully serene,
Where sudden shadows stirred and fled unseen
And mellow orange lights revealed the street
Or glimmered vaguely on the stealthy cars.
And in the moon-lit lawns of heaven, the stars
Like daisies were. And thoughts with tender wings
Brushed past and sang of young unsullied things.

SOLLIES VILLE, PROVENCE [EXTRACT][21]

Below, the dimpled valley wanders down
And all its farms and happy fields lay bare;
But here are crumbling walls against the sky,
Whose mournful windows stare
Like eyes oppressed by age-long memories,
And 'mid the silver-flashing olive trees,
The brown-roofed houses seem
A flock of huddled sheep, seen in a dream.

---

[21] This extract from an otherwise unpublished and unknown poem appeared in a 1922 article by Harihar Das on 'The Poetry of Dorothy Noel Bonarjee'.

SENSE OF LOVE AND LOSS

[YOU SAID ONCE I WAS LUCKY][22]

You said once I was lucky, but you wouldn't say it now;
   You swore that fortune never came your way;
You used to say I always scored – well, now your turn is here
   You must confess that you have won today.

I've read your letter once again, you write that you're "just off,"
   And wish that I were with you doing the same.
You mention "my commission" – Oh! the fates have smiled at last
   And you, not I, are scoring in this game.

They say that I am shirking, that my duty is out there;
   They talk a lot – I wonder if they know
That we who have to stay at home, aren't finding it all fun;
   The easier job would be to cut and go.

---

[22] *The Dragon*, December 1914

MORNING[23]

Through morning fields of dewiness
On joyful feet we laughing went,
And felt the young day's shy caress,
And cool wind-fingers steal
Across our eyes ... ineffably content.
But when I kissed your lips, you cried
And passionately said
"When we are dead
We shall no longer feel
This warm refulgent tide
Thrill our responding bodies so;
But our sad spirits wandering
Will never know
The summer's languid breath, the tingling mirth
Of waves that break in splendid showers,
The silken touch of flowers
And bloomy fruit, the smell of earth.
And oh!" – you sorrowfully said –
"How I shall miss
(A poor insensuous spirit lover-wise)
Your hands to touch, your lips to kiss,
Your quiet friendly eyes." –
                    And now you're dead.

---

[23] *Welsh Outlook*, July 1919. Also entitled 'Gloria Mundi', perhaps from the Latin phrase 'sic transit gloria mundi' or 'thus passes earthly glory'.

RENUNCIATION[24]

So I must give thee up – not with the glow
Of those who losing much yet rather gain.
But losing all. Did never martyr go
Along the bleeding road of useless pain?
Did never one held prisoner by a creed,
Obsessed by stern heroic ghosts, made dumb
By those who answered duty to his need,
With faithless loathing feet to his fate come?
And die with hate in his young tortured eyes?
And mock with sceptical pain-twisted lips
His wasted hideous doom? So mocking dies
My god-like flaming joy beneath the whips
Of analysing thought. O Heart denied!
Now must thou take what barren thought can give.
And thou O Body scourged, be satisfied
Through miser-fears on fallen crumbs to live.

---

[24] *Welsh Outlook*, November 1919. This appears to be the poem to which a handwritten note by Dorothy Bonarjee refers: 'Written at the age of 22 when a Welsh student after 3 years of secret engagement dropped me because his parents said "She is very beautiful and intelligent but she is Indian." / A bit overcharged with adjectives but that was then the fashion of the day.'

DE AMICITIA INVENTATIS[25]

This morning when the dawn was scarce awake
With dew-shod feet we crept down to the sea
Through dim half-haunted fields; we could not shake
Sleep's veil aside, nor dawn's pale wizardry
Ensnared we sped down where the white sands lie
Adventurous eyed and joyous – You and I
Today and Yesterday – oh flowering days!
And ardent sky, tomorrow fair as these;
What gracious hours of laughter and light words
With deep unreasoned happiness ablaze.
Now is the sunset faint behind frail trees;
And soon like driven flocks of shining birds
Reluctant night her myriad stars will bring
And our glad hours climb to them wing on wing.

---

[25] The title can be translated as 'On Friendship Discovered'. Cicero wrote a famous treatise 'De Amicitia' or 'On Friendship'. Inscribed 'To Neil', Dorothy's younger brother

THE ENCHANTED GARDEN

Soft sloping lawns as secret in the night
As green mist-laden seas;
And shadowy trees
  Whose branches bending low
  Curve like protecting wings
About the earth; and roses dimly white
Pale stars that glow
(And die) enthralled by mute immortal yearnings.

When all the world is still and wrapt in sleep
  The enchanted garden waits for us alone ...
We'll say no word
But hand in hand we'll walk the paths that lead
Past the dark hedges where the night is deep,
  To where the roses stirred;
  And petals softly blown
Fell trembling on the grass for their heart's need

Ah! see them fall ...
  Was that a singing bird?
Or just my heart that listening listening hears
  The call?

Your arms hold all my shelters, all my dreams
There lies my enchanted garden, there my joy.
Night's mystery, and life and death all seem
Burned by your lips to gold without alloy.
Beneath your touch, dear love, I am the rose
Whose life and scent and beauty yearns to you.
  Whose trembling heart but knows
  The great need to be true.

ARROGANCE

We loved so splendidly in that great hour
That life and death knew nothing of our power
And when we kissed, I laughed because at last
I stood where God had never passed.

But when your little frightened soul had fled
And all your glorious radiant lies were dead
I laughed again because you knew I fell
Where God had never passed – in hell.

THE REALIST

  And so the days will go
  The lost relentless days;
  Each one more slow
  And I, poor fool, will gaze
Upon your photograph with twitching eyes,
And clench my hands and bite my twisted lips
And feel the savage tears like stinging whips
And laugh to see how soon my courage dies.

  And so the days will go
  When I am left alone –
  Each one more slow
  With bitter hours sown.
I will not whine – I say I will not whine
Like any beaten dog that howls for pain –
And yet – O God that he were here again
For one short moment with his hand on mine.

DISCONTENT

I sometimes wonder when I see your eyes
So cool and pitiful and sadly wise
If you have guessed the truth and hide your pain
And when you dimly smile and shake your head
And leave my blind sick passionate words unsaid
I think your white proud soul is almost slain.
Oh I am happy, yet my spirit sleeps
Wrapt round in happiness, through tranquil days.

My dull mind in this ordered garden strays
And in my blood a deadening languor creeps
Dear, think not that my love has seemed to fail
But I am dead and stale, and I would see
Unquiet lands and live uncertainly
And find wild thoughts my drowsy heart assail.

THE IDEALIST

"Go now they say, go now and save mankind
O God of love. Not as thou once didst go
With preparation steeled, but wholly blind
Not victim for an ordained sacrifice
But hurled to unpremeditated woe
Drink now the cup, without thy Godhead's aid
As men must drink; by man and man alone
Not God's man; and pay whatever price
Thou makest them pay for everlasting joy
Go now and save the world ere it has strayed
Too far from thee and turned its heart to stone."

So speak my flame eyed angels mockingly
And I have said no word – what can I say?
Whose bitter eyes have watched my glory die
On whose heart lies the weight of centuries.
A Dreamer, impotent to save – or slay
I grow too old, I cannot leave my dreams
For those remote remembered agonies
Once I was young. The youth is ever bold
When dreams are fire, a little thing it seems
To suffer shame and curse, to save all man.
To build the new and overthrow the old.
To talk of love and faith – comes age, and then –
"O ye of little faith" I bravely said
And now my faith like thine is almost dead.

TRIOLET

Since we must love why have it so
   Give me your mouth and let me drink
For love and hate together go
   Since we must love why have it so
And let our wiser bodies show
   Our warring minds love's golden link
Since we must love who have it so
   Give me your mouth and let me drink

SONGS TO CLAIRE-AWUNA[26]

The world is full of lovely things;
Of birds with shining painted wings;
Of friendly dogs that bark, and goats
That let me touch their hairy coats.

The world's so full of joy and light
That I'm quite sorry when it's night;
When Mummy baths me till I'm new.
I love my bath – and Mummy too.

When Claire Awuna walks abroad
There's magic in the world.
For every flower's a jewel bright,
Each leaf a flag unfurled.

Each stone becomes a *special* stone
That I must marvel at.
The hens become heroic birds
And sweetly sings each gnat.

The happy sun goes on his way;
The happy hours rejoice.
And Claire-Awuna laughs aloud
To hear her happy voice

---

[26] Claire-Aruna Surtel was Dorothy Bonarjee's daughter.

TO AMIEN DE MEMPSON[27]

I had a little son whose eyes were bright
With love and joy – perhaps with sorrow too
And yours are full of gentleness and light –
He died I think because he missed God's smile
As babies sometimes do –
And when you laugh and toss your sunny hair
Or leave your splendid play to dream awhile
Of lovely coloured things – I like to think
That you and he were friends in heaven – or why
Should I so love your happy voice – and see
My little laughing son look up at me.

---

[27] Dorothy Bonarjee's son, Denis Surtel, died in infancy.

ACKNOWLEDGEMENTS

Sheela Bonarjee has made it her mission to secure recognition for the remarkable life and achievements of her Auntie Dorf and to gain a wider audience for her poetry. This book would not have happened without the care with which Sheela kept her aunt's papers and the zeal with which she promoted Dorf's reputation as a poet. She has become a close and treasured friend. We have also benefitted from the encouragement, support and hospitality of Sheela's daughter and son-in-law, Shali and Chris Bullough.

We are grateful to Honno – and particularly to Jane Aaron, the editor of the Honno Classics series – for embracing the idea of this book and seeing it through to publication. It's a real thrill to see Dorothy Bonarjee take her place among Honno's distinguished roll-call of Welsh women writers.

We hugely appreciate the expertise and support of scholars, archivists and producers who have been generous with their advice and encouragement. Susan J. Davies and Faaeza Jasdanwalla-Williams have given unfailing support and expert counsel. We also wish to express warm thanks to Catrin M.S. Davies, Ruth Evans, Eluned Gramich, Mererid Hopwood, Beth Jenkins, Aled Jones, Elin Haf Gruffydd Jones, and Sumita Mukherjee.

Photographs and images are published with the kind permission of Sheela Bonarjee, except the photograph of Dorothy Bonarjee with women fellow students at Aberystwyth which is held at Aberystwyth University Archives, and is included with their permission.

A NOTE ABOUT THE EDITORS

Mohini Gupta is a DPhil candidate at the Faculty of Asian and Middle Eastern Studies, University of Oxford. She was selected as the Charles Wallace India Trust Translator-Writer Fellow in 2017 for creative writing and translation, hosted by Literature Across Frontiers at the University of Aberystwyth. Her English-Hindi translations have been published by Tulika Publishers, and she regularly speaks and writes on languages, literature and translation. She is a Welsh-language learner and enthusiast.

Andrew Whitehead is a historian and journalist, a former BBC India correspondent and an honorary professor at the University of Nottingham. He was for many years an editor and is now an associate editor of *History Workshop Journal*. Andrew has written a biography of Freda Bedi (née Houlston), a woman who, in the 1930s, travelled in the other direction from Dorothy Bonarjee, from England to India where she became a prominent nationalist and leftist and a pioneering woman journalist before turning to Tibetan Buddhism and becoming a Buddhist nun.